Animal Jokes

Joe King

Abdo Kids Junior
is an Imprint of Abdo Kids
abdobooks.com

abdobooks.com

Published by Abdo Kids, a division of ABDO, P.O. Box 398166, Minneapolis, Minnesota 55439.
Copyright © 2022 by Abdo Consulting Group, Inc. International copyrights reserved in all countries.
No part of this book may be reproduced in any form without written permission from the publisher.
Abdo Kids Junior™ is a trademark and logo of Abdo Kids.

Printed in the United States of America, North Mankato, Minnesota.

102021

012022

THIS BOOK CONTAINS
RECYCLED MATERIALS

Photo Credits: iStock, Shutterstock

Production Contributors: Teddy Borth, Jennie Forsberg, Grace Hansen

Design Contributors: Candice Keimig, Pakou Moua

Library of Congress Control Number: 2021940315
Publisher's Cataloging-in-Publication Data

Names: King, Joe, author.

Title: Animal jokes / by Joe King

Description: Minneapolis, Minnesota : Abdo Kids, 2022 | Series: Abdo kids jokes | Includes online resource.

Identifiers: ISBN 9781098209162 (lib. bdg.) | ISBN 9781644946305 (pbk.) | ISBN 9781098209865 (ebook)
   | ISBN 9781098260224 (Read-to-Me ebook)

Subjects: LCSH: Jokes--Juvenile literature. | Wit and humor--Juvenile literature. | Animals--Juvenile
   literature.

Classification: DDC 818.602--dc23

Table of Contents

Animal Jokes

What do cows like to drink?

Oreo smoooo-thies!

Why did the chicken cross the park?

To get to the other slide!

4

What do you call the horse
that just moved in next door?
Your new neiiiiiiighhh-bor.
HA!
HAY!
HA!
NEIGH!
5

How do you stop a bull
from charging?

You unplug it!

How can you tell which
rabbits are getting old?

Look for the gray hares!

Where do sheep go
on vacation?
The Baaa-hamas.
Ba!
Ba!

Why can't you play hockey with pigs?

They always hog the puck!

What do you call a pig that knows karate?

A pork chop!

Ha! Ha! Ha!
Why can't you trust a pig with a secret?
Because it will squeal!
9

If a seagull flies over the sea,
what flies over the bay?

A bagel!

What do you call a duck
that gets all A's?

*A **wise** quacker.*

LOL!
What do you call two birds in love?
Tweethearts!
AWW! SWEET!

What animal can you always
find at a baseball game?

A bat!

Why don't snails like
fast food?

Because they can't catch it!

What is black and white, and looks like a penguin?

A penguin.

How do you make an octopus laugh?

With ten tickles!

What do sharks say when something cool happens?

Jawsome!

Why don't sharks eat clownfish?
Because they taste funny!
Chews Wisely!
TEE! HEE!
15

What kind of haircuts
do bees get?

Buzzzzzcuts.

Why do bees have
sticky hair?

They use a honeycomb.

16

What do you get when you cross a centipede with a parrot?
A walkie talkie.
SQUAW!
HA!
AHH!
+
17

Why didn't the teddy bear
eat his dessert?

Because he was stuffed.

What do you call a bear
with no teeth?

A gummy bear.

18

What did the wolf say when it stubbed its toe?
Owwwww-ch!
OWW!
HOWWW!
FUNNY!
19

What happened when the frog parked in the no-parking zone?

His car got toad away!

What do you call a funny snake?

Hissssssterical!

20

What do you call an alligator that solves crimes?

An investigator!

INSPECTOR CHOMPY!

A-HA!

Joke-Telling Tips!
• Know your audience
• Timing is everything
• Confidence is key
• Go out on a high note!
22

Glossary

pun

a joke using a word that sounds like a different word or has another meaning. Examples from this book are "ten tickles" (tentacles) and "tweethearts" (sweethearts).

wise

having an understanding about what is true or good.

Index

Abdo Kids ONLINE
FREE! ONLINE MULTIMEDIA RESOURCES

Visit **abdokids.com** to access crafts, games, videos, and more!